Earth's Environment in Danger

Loss of Biodiversity

Rachael Hames

PowerKiDS press

New York

Published in 2018 by The Rosen Publishing Group, Inc.
29 East 21st Street, New York, NY 10010

First Edition

Editor: Elizabeth Krajnik
Book Design: Rachel Rising

Photo Credits: Cover Shirokuma/a.collectionRF/Getty Images; Cover. pp. 1, 3, 4, 6, 8, 10, 11, 12, 14, 16, 18, 20, 22, 23, 24 ALKRO/Shutterstock.com; p . 4 Christoph Burgstedt/Shutterstock.com; p. 5,10 Ethan Daniels/Shutterstock.com; p. 7 Harry Beugelink/Shutterstock.com; p. 8 Yulia Moiseeva/Shutterstock.com; p. 9 (top) Dmitry Polonskiy/Shutterstock.com; p. 9 (middle) Vlad61/Shutterstock.com; p. 9 (bottom) Happy monkey/Shutterstock.com; p. 11 seamuss/Shutterstock.com; p. 11 seeyah panwan/Shutterstock.com; p. 13 (top) Matej Valocky/Shutterstock.com; p. 13 (middle) Tanja_G/Shutterstock.com; p. 13 (bottom) Lev Kropotov/Shutterstock.com; p. 14 Den Edryshov/Shutterstock.com;p. 15 Pavlo Baliukh/Shutterstock.com; p. 17 Michael & Patricia Fogden/Minden Pictures/Getty Images; p. 19 (top) Georgette Douwma/Nature Picture Library/Getty Images; p. 19 (bottom) buttchi 3 Sha Life/Shutterstock.com; p. 21 Naufal MQ/Shutterstock.com; p. 22 Bika Ambon/Shutterstock.com.

Cataloging-in-Publication Data

Names: Hames, Rachael.
Title: Loss of biodiversity / Rachael Hames.
Description: New York : PowerKids Press, 2018. | Series: Earth's environment in danger | Includes index.
Identifiers: ISBN 9781538326091 (pbk.) | ISBN 9781538325391 (library bound) | ISBN 9781538326107 (6 pack)
Subjects: LCSH: Biodiversity–Juvenile literature. | Biodiversity conservation–Juvenile literature. | Nature–Effect of human beings on–Juvenile literature.
Classification: LCC QH541.15.B56 H36 2018 | DDC 333.95–dc23

Manufactured in the United States of America

CPSIA Compliance Information: Batch #BW18PK: For Further Information contact Rosen Publishing, New York, New York at 1-800-237-9932

Contents

What Is Biodiversity?

Biodiversity is the existence of many different species, or kinds, of plants and animals in an **environment**. Almost everywhere you look, there's biodiversity. Biodiversity can be studied on many levels. On a large scale, our entire planet is full of biodiversity. On a smaller scale, you can look at the biodiversity in your backyard.

All the species in one **ecosystem** depend on each other. Imagine your backyard. What do you see? There may be a few trees, grass, flowers, birds, and maybe some squirrels. However, biodiversity goes beyond the things you can see. Biodiversity exists on the **microscopic** level, too.

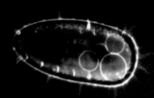
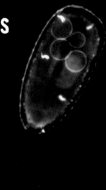
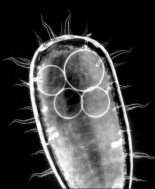

microscopic organisms

Biodiversity doesn't just exist on land. Earth's bodies of water are home to many different species of plants, animals, and bacteria. Compare this healthy coral to the dead coral on the cover. Can you see the differences?

Types of Biodiversity

There are three different types of biodiversity: **genetic** diversity, species diversity, and ecosystem diversity. These three types of biodiversity must exist to keep the Earth's ecosystems balanced.

Genetic diversity refers to the genetic differences within one species. For example, there are a number of species of dogs. However, not all dogs look the same. This is because they have different genes.

Species diversity is the **variety** of species within one habitat, or the natural home for plants, animals, and other living things. This is what most people think of when they hear the term "biodiversity."

[Danger Alert!]

Scientists have found that modern alpine chipmunks have less genetic diversity than alpine chipmunks that lived many years ago. One of the biggest causes of this decrease in genetic diversity is **climate change**. Alpine chipmunks are easily affected by changes in temperature.

Increased temperatures caused by climate change have forced the alpine chipmunk to live higher in the Sierra Nevada Mountains in California. Today, the alpine chipmunk is in danger of **extinction**.

7

Ecosystem diversity refers to the variety of ecosystems on our planet. Earth has deserts, mountains, grasslands, oceans, and many other types of ecosystems. How these different ecosystems interact with the living and nonliving things within them is very important. Without ecosystems, species wouldn't have a place to live and **evolve**.

Without a variety of ecosystems, Earth would be a very different place. Can you imagine life on Earth without forests? Without forests, we wouldn't have clean air to breathe, and many plant and animal species wouldn't have homes.

ecosystem diversity

species diversity

genetic diversity

9

Biodiversity Around the World

Biodiversity exists in every ecosystem on Earth. However, some areas have much more biodiversity than others. For example, there's more biodiversity in areas where it's warm year round than there is in areas that have warm summers and cold winters. Mountain and desert areas have even less biodiversity.

[Danger Alert!]

The Coral Triangle is home to about 600 species of **reef**-building corals, six of the world's seven **marine** turtle species, and more than 2,000 species of reef fish. However, all of these species are in danger of dying out due to human activities.

ASIA

PHILIPPINES

More than 120 million
people living in the Coral
Triangle, highlighted orange,
depend on **resources** from
the area. If the species in
the Coral Triangle die, these
people will no longer have
food or jobs.

BRUNEI
MALAYSIA

INDONESIA

PAPUA NEW
GUINEA

TIMOR-LESTE

INDIAN OCEAN

AUSTRALIA

Some of the places with the most
biodiversity on Earth are the western Pacific
and Indian Oceans and the Amazon rain
forest. The Amazon rain forest is home to at
least 40,000 species of plants. One of the
ocean regions with the most biodiversity is the
Coral Triangle in the western Pacific Ocean.

Why Is Biodiversity Important?

All species on Earth depend on each other. Think of it almost like a food web, but on a larger scale—a life web. Biodiversity is important to all life-forms. When there is greater genetic biodiversity, species are more likely to respond positively to changes in their environment.

Humans also benefit from biodiversity. We depend on a wide variety of species of plants, animals, and **fungi** for food, clothing, fuel, building supplies, and even medicines.

However, one of the most important parts of biodiversity is how species interact with and depend on one another. If one species dies out, it could lead to many other species dying out.

[Danger Alert!]

Honeybees play an important role in pollination, which is the process of taking pollen from one flower, plant, or tree to another. In recent years, the honeybee population has been decreasing. This could lead to certain crops being unable to reproduce, which leads to a loss of biodiversity.

Humans benefit from plant biodiversity in many ways. Plants give us clean air to breathe and food to eat. Humans use plants to make medicines, clothing, and building supplies.

Threats to Biodiversity

In recent years, scientists have seen a major decrease in biodiversity. This decrease has indirect and direct causes, but almost all of these causes are due to human activity.

The need for food and energy leads to humans overusing resources. Earth's habitats begin to change and may no longer be able to support life. Large amounts of certain chemicals may pollute ecosystems and harm the life-forms there. Humans may purposely or accidentally introduce **invasive species** to an ecosystem. Climate change also **threatens** biodiversity.

Biodiversity is very important to most countries. Without it, these countries could suffer greatly.

One of the biggest threats to marine biodiversity is overfishing. Overfishing decreases the number of fish in the ocean. It's hard to tell just how quickly the world's oceans are losing biodiversity because many ocean species haven't been discovered yet.

Case Study: The Golden Toad

Some scientists consider the golden toad of Costa Rica the first animal to go extinct as a direct result of climate change. This amphibian disappeared in 1989. Since then, the golden toad has been used as proof of biodiversity loss and to show the general public the consequences of climate change.

Not many people completely understand how an animal goes extinct. Several issues led to the toad's extinction: droughts, sickness, and environmental damage. Scientists aren't able to find one exact cause for the golden toad's extinction. However, the story of this species of toad is often used as a tool to educate people about **conservation**.

After it was discovered in the Monteverde region of Costa Rica in 1964, the golden toad became an important conservation species to scientists. It had a very small population, and it lived in a very small area. In 1972, scientists set up a small, protected area to try to keep the toads safe.

Halting the Loss of Biodiversity

Human activities are the reason for much biodiversity loss. This means humans need to change the way they do certain things to keep biodiversity at a healthy level. For instance, one of the biggest causes of habitat loss and loss of biodiversity is deforestation to make room for growing crops and raising livestock.

Another way to keep a healthy level of biodiversity is to find biodiversity hot spots. Then we can work hard to keep the species living there safe from harm. The Great Barrier Reef in the Coral Sea off the coast of Queensland, Australia, and the Amazon rain forest in South America are two biodiversity hot spots.

[Danger Alert!]

The Great Barrier Reef brings the area more than $6 billion from tourism each year. However, the reef's corals are dying off at an alarming rate. If something isn't done to save them, the animals living in and around the reef will also die out and the tourism industry will suffer.

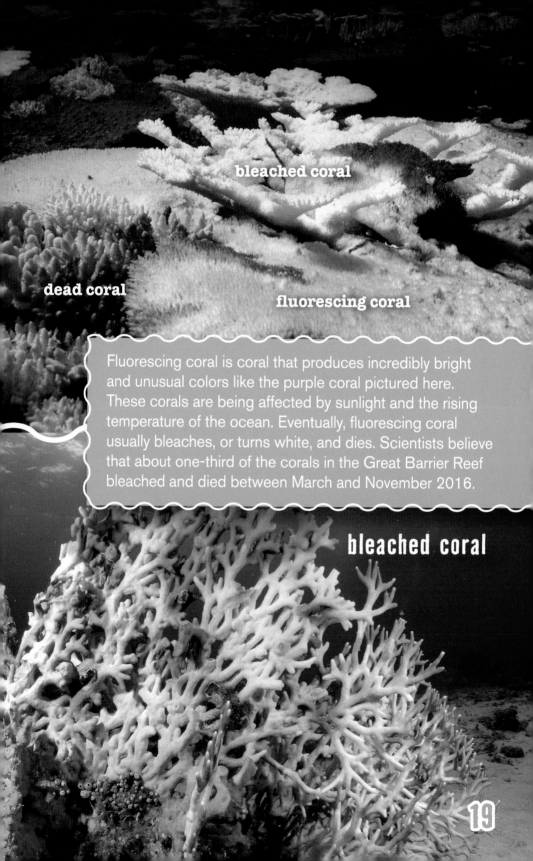

bleached coral

dead coral

fluorescing coral

Fluorescing coral is coral that produces incredibly bright and unusual colors like the purple coral pictured here. These corals are being affected by sunlight and the rising temperature of the ocean. Eventually, fluorescing coral usually bleaches, or turns white, and dies. Scientists believe that about one-third of the corals in the Great Barrier Reef bleached and died between March and November 2016.

bleached coral

Legislation to Protect Biodiversity

Many countries around the world have adopted **legislation** with the goal of protecting the planet's biodiversity. One example is the Endangered Species Act in the United States. Passed by Congress in 1973, this law protects about 2,000 species from threats posed by human activities. Other countries, such as the United Kingdom and Australia, have adopted similar legislation.

One other way the government can act to keep biodiversity at a healthy level is to create wildlife preserves and conservation areas. In the United States, the National Park Service (NPS) works to preserve biodiversity by restoring ecosystems and controlling invasive species and pests.

[Danger Alert!]

Yellowstone became the country's first official national park in 1872. This park is located in the states of Wyoming, Montana, and Idaho. The NPS was created in 1916. Without the NPS's efforts, the United States would likely look very different.

The United Nations Educational, Scientific, and Cultural Organization (UNESCO) World Heritage Site program helps preserve biodiversity by recognizing areas of particular importance, such as the Western Ghats mountain chain in India.

Western Ghats, Kodaikanal, Tamil Nadu, India

What Can You Do?

You can help stop—and maybe even reverse—biodiversity loss by making small changes in your daily choices. Making an effort to decrease your use of electricity, gasoline, and other harmful energy sources can help slow down climate change.

Buying wood that has come from a responsible, legal source can help reduce deforestation. Buying seafood from a responsible source can help prevent biodiversity loss in Earth's oceans.

If you go on vacation, make sure you don't buy anything made from the skin, fur, bone, shell, beak, or hooves of an endangered species. Reducing the market for these items may help prevent endangered species from going extinct.

climate change: Change in Earth's weather caused by human activity.

conservation: Efforts to care for the natural world.

ecosystem: A natural community of living and nonliving things.

environment: The conditions that surround a living thing and affect the way it lives.

evolve: To grow and change over time.

extinction: The state of no longer existing.

fungus: A living thing that is like a plant but that doesn't have leaves, flowers, or green color or make its own food. The plural form is fungi.

genetic: Having to do with genes, or the parts of cells that control the appearance, growth, and other traits of a living thing.

invasive species: Plants or animals from one area that spread quickly in a new area and harm native plants and animals.

legislation: A law or set of laws made by a government.

marine: Of or relating to the sea.

microscopic: So small it can only be seen with a microscope.

reef: A chain of rocks or coral or a ridge of sand at or near the surface of the water.

resource: Something that can be used.

threaten: To show an intention to do harm or something unwanted.

variety: The state of having many different things.

Websites

Due to the changing nature of Internet links, PowerKids Press has
developed an online list of websites related to the subject of this book.
This site is updated regularly. Please use this link to access the list:
www.powerkidslinks.com/eeid/bio